The Majesty of Beaufort

The Majesty of
BEAUFORT

Photography and Text by
Nancy Easter White

Foreword by
John Ellington White

PELICAN PUBLISHING COMPANY
Gretna 2000

Library of Congress Cataloging in Publication Data

White, Nancy E.
    The Majesty of Beaufort / text and photography by Nancy E. White ; foreword by
John Ellington White.
       p. cm.
    ISBN 1-56554-720-9 (alk. paper)
    1. Historic buildings—South Carolina—Beaufort—Pictorial works. 2. Beaufort
(S.C.)—History—Pictorial works. 3. Beaufort (S.C.)—Buildings, structures, etc.—
Pictorial works. 4. Architecture—South Carolina—Beaufort—Pictorial works. I. Title.

F279.B3 W53 2000
975.7'99—dc21

00-038527

Printed in Hong Kong
Published by Pelican Publishing Company, Inc.
1000 Burmaster Street, Gretna, Louisiana 70053

CONTENTS

FOREWORD

Looking at our city through the prism of a bright summer morning, one could easily imagine that it had just been towed in from the sea by a school of dolphins and placed on a bend in the Beaufort River where everybody would notice it—this shining gift from the deep ocean.

But Beaufort is not as youthful as it appears, having been around since 1521 when Spanish explorers first set foot on those shores. Since then it has passed through a number of hands—French (1562), Scottish (1624), and English (1670), whose hands seemed to have been the strongest since they held onto it the longest. Some of them, in fact, are still here. A couple of British soldiers from the Revolutionary War are buried in the cemetery of Beaufort's oldest church, St. Helena's. The English returned to Beaufort for the War of 1812.

Wars have been drawn to Beaufort for some reason, but none of them made as deep and lasting an impression as the Civil War. Beaufort was an occupied city during this conflict. Union soldiers had their pictures taken in front of the same buildings and houses that the present generation passes each day.

If you want to see evidence of these soldiers, climb the front stairs of the George Elliott House, which was a Union hospital, and gaze upon a wall on the second floor where soldiers from New York and Massachusetts and Pennsylvania, boys a long way from home, left their names ("Elias Brody," "Franklin Wise" . . .), the dates they were here—"June, 1862"—and even how they were feeling on a summer day in the steamy, unairconditioned Low Country of South Carolina: "sons offa bitch," a misspelled sentiment that goes straight to the heart.

History ennobles whatever it touches. It says, "Look at me. After all I've been through, I am still here."

History leaves an unmistakable "patina," a depth, a presence that Nancy Easter White has captured in these wonderful photographs. They are a pleasure to behold as well as a tribute to a beautiful place. The authenticity of Time resides within the borders of each. "We are the real thing," they tell us—the real houses, the real buildings of a city chosen by dolphins on a bend of the Beaufort River.

John Ellington White

The Majesty of Beaufort

DOWNTOWN HISTORIC DISTRICT

John Mark Verdier House
801 Bay Street

Beaufort's waterways were explored by the Spanish as early as 1520, and the French tried to settle in the Sea Islands sometime around 1562, but the town of Beaufort did not exist until the early 18th century. Indians were a constant threat until they were finally subdued in 1715, during the Yemassee Indian War. An enterprising Beaufort merchant built the John Mark Verdier House, at 801 Bay Street, in 1790. A two-story frame structure on a raised tabby basement, the house is of the Federal period but displays Adam-style refinements on the interior and exterior. The doorway is a masterpiece of delicate carving above and surrounding the semi-elliptical fanlight. Inside, open to the public for tours, are gracefully proportioned rooms and Adams-style mantels.

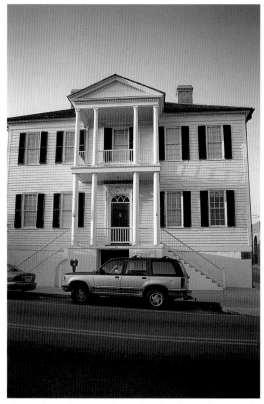

It is often called the "Lafayette House" because local tradition maintains that the Marquis de Lafayette spoke from the portico on his American tour in 1825. The house fell into a steep decline after Union occupation of the town during the 1860s and was condemned in 1942. A group of citizens banded together to save it from destruction, eventually forming the Historic Beaufort Foundation. They finally acquired the house in 1955, and completed its restoration in 1976. The Foundation opens the historic house for tours daily.

A well-to-do merchant built the John Mark Verdier House in 1805. A raised double portico dominates the front façade and identifies it as a fine example of the Early Classical Revival style.

George Parsons Elliott House

1001 Bay Street

Construction of the George Parsons Elliott House is attributed to its name-sake, in 1840. The two-story, framed dwelling is raised on an elevated tabby basement. (Tabby, a precursor to modern concrete, is a composite of lime, sand, water, and oyster shells.) The entrance, facing south, is on a porch raised on brick piers. Four unfluted Doric columns dominate this façade, as does the dramatic balustrade of wrought and cast iron. The upper porch, added in 1875, displays turned balusters, which are repeated as a parapet to the porch roof.

The George Elliott House was sold to Dr. William J. Jenkins of Land's End Plantation on St. Helena Island just before the beginning of the Civil War. Abandoned during the conflict, the mansion was purchased by George Holmes at a direct tax commission sale. Holmes' wife, Julia Hazel Holmes, lived in the house until her death in the 1930s.

The main entrance porch, which faces south toward the Beaufort River, has a striking balustrade made of cast and wrought iron.

Lovely plantings accent the fence bordering the property along Bay Street.

Visible on the second floor landing are doodles left by Civil War soldiers.

Until recently, the Elliott House was used for commercial offices. It is now a private residence.

The front hall, seen from the opposite side as the photograph at left, looking down from the stairway.

An upstairs dining room is elegantly spare. Views from the windows look onto Beaufort's downtown commercial district.

Beaufort Arsenal
713 Craven Street

Its vivid yellow flat roof and bold crenelations distinguish the Beaufort Arsenal at 713 Craven Street. Built in 1795, rebuilt in 1852, and enlarged in a 1943 Works Progress Administration project, the facility now houses the Beaufort Museum. Its military affiliation is with the Beaufort Volunteer Artillery, once the military might of the town.

Behind the pointed arch gateway are five antique cannons, including a bronze, 24-pound field howitzer that was used on the *U.S.S. George Washington,* an Army vessel operating in the Beaufort area in the 19th cen-

tury. A Confederate battery sank the *George Washington* on April 9, 1865. Local lore has it that many years later, a man catching crabs spotted the sunken relic. After knocking away oyster shells, he recognized the historically significant cannon. He notified authorities in Beaufort, who raised the piece and displayed it in the Arsenal.

The courtyard of the Beaufort Arsenal is the site of occasional Civil War reenactments. Participants "make camp" within the Arsenal walls, giving instruction in history and entertaining visitors with their amazingly realistic depiction of wartime life.

Although historically accurate, the yellow paint of the Arsenal caused a stir when applied a few years ago during restoration efforts.

Five Civil War cannons are on permanent display at the museum. The collection includes two wrought-iron field rifles, two cast-iron rifled Blakelys, and the bronze field howitzer.

Massive pointed-arch gates open onto a walled courtyard. The lancet windows of the main structure echo the military theme.

St. Helena's Episcopal Church
501 Church Street

Two important things dominated plantation life in the 18th century: work and religion. The Episcopal faith was the religion of choice among the

wealthy planter class. Therefore St. Helena's Parish wielded enormous power among the early settlers of Beaufort. Participants had the knowledge and the means to bring sophisticated architecture to the Low Country. St. Helena's, in downtown Beaufort, was the physical mother to many outlying chapels. The church was organized in 1712 and built in 1724 of bricks brought over from England.

One of the oldest churches in America, the brick structure is coated with a layer of pink stucco. Its interior is elaborately appointed with elegant shutters and columns. An upper galley once provided space for slave worshippers. In 1999, the aging church went through an elaborate restoration. Huge cables were tightened slowly across the entire building to straighten the leaning walls.

Covered by a stucco veneer, the brick walls of St. Helena's have offered invisible service as the structural foundation of the building for over a hundred years. Thousands of worshippers have walked this gracious path to worship within the venerable building.

Tombstones in the church's graveyard were used as operating tables during the Civil War.

Many of Beaufort's oldest and most recognizable family names are represented in the cemetery at St. Helena's.

This brick path is used by parishioners summoned to worship from Sunday school in the Parish House, located across the street.

A detail of delicate iron fencing surrounding a burial site.

St. Helena's stucco covering over brick is scored to resemble stone. The building underwent a multi-million-dollar restoration in 1999.

Early settlers to the Beaufort area brought with them knowledge of sophisticated classical architecture. Plaques attached to the walls describe the history of the church.

The beautiful church, surrounded by a high brick wall which encloses an old graveyard, is a landmark of the historic town.

Frederick Fraser House

901 Prince Street

Frederick Grimke Fraser of Huspah Plantation built the Frederick Fraser House, 901 Prince Street, of brick and tabby in 1803-1804. It was common in the 19th century for planters to have a home near their plantations and another in town, traveling between the two. Some of the most distinguishing features of this impressive mansion include the wonderful, wide double stairs leading to the main entrance, the twelve slender columns supporting double verandahs, and the Palladian-style doorway, which opens onto the second floor verandah. The house is now home to a couple who are avid gardeners. The husband has turned this hobby into a second career, designing formal gardens for friends and clients. Plantings surround the house with nearly year-round color.

The Frederick Fraser House incorporates many details from the Adam style of architecture, including the Palladian window on the second floor verandah.

The circa 1860 double gates, which lead into the yard, are from the historic First Presbyterian Church in York, South Carolina. The current owner, who grew up in York, saved these gates for more than 40 years waiting for the perfect use.

The gilt mirror in the front hall is a sentimental favorite of the owners. It was a gift from the husband's father to his daughter-in-law. It is rumored to have come from the Italian embassy in Washington, D.C. The chandelier hanging here was a 25th wedding anniversary gift between the owners.

Gardening is a passion of the home's owners. The formal design complements the home and provides beautiful foliage and flowers nearly year-round. The antique gates are from the owner's home in York.

An upstairs bedroom is furnished with a circa 1860 Victorian bed, armoire, tables, and dresser that were passed to the owners from parents, grandparents, and great-grandparents. The bowl and pitcher set belonged to the husband's grandmother.

The portraits in the dining room are of ancestors James Harvey Witherspoon and his wife, Jane Donnom Witherspoon. The mirror over the fireplace is a family heirloom that once hung in the library of the husband's childhood home. The cut glass pieces are part of his mother's collection. All of the furnishings are family pieces.

The living room is filled with antiques passed down from family members. The portrait is of the wife's great-great-grandfather James Wardlaw.

A view of Wesley United Methodist Church from a second floor bedroom.

The second floor landing from the inside looking out. Afternoon light pours through the historic door to the Oriental rug inside.

John A. Cuthbert House, "Cuthbert House Inn"

1203 Bay Street

This fine home, now a popular inn, graces the downtown district with its monumental presence. Construction details reveal that the front portion of the house was built sometime around 1810. Significant remodeling probably occurred in the late 1830s or early 1840s. Inside, visitors will find fine Federal-style molding, a marble fireplace, and many graceful appointments. Sold at auction after the Civil War, the home passed into the ownership of Union Gen. Rufus Saxton. Saxton then sold the house to his friend Duncan Wilson in 1882. Wilson may have been responsible for the Victorian-style gingerbread trim and extensions to the south porch.

Woodwork in the entrance hall is of the Federal style. An arched opening offers a glimpse of the winding stair to the second floor guestrooms.

The Cuthbert House faces the Beaufort River on Bay Street.

Fanciful lace curtains reveal the view across the front porch to the river beyond.

Owners of the inn have spent years collecting the antiques that fill these rooms.

Looking through the antebellum doorways on the first floor offers a visual delight.

Guests of the inn have private tables in the cozy dining room. The owners decorate the tables with seasonal flowers from their garden.

Afternoon light floods an upstairs bedroom, where guests receive the royal treatment.

Thomas Moore Rhett House,
"The Rhett House Inn"

1009 Craven Street

The builder of the Thomas Moore Rhett House is unknown, but construction clues date the house to about 1820. Historians know that namesake Thomas Rhett and his wife, Caroline Barnwell, owned this two-story, Federal-style mansion just prior to the Civil War. Today it houses the only four-star, four-diamond inn in town. The dwelling is raised on a masonry basement and fronted by a Greek Revival-style porch on the south and west façades. Visitors to the Rhett House climb elliptical stairs to the first floor. The main entrance faces south toward the Beaufort River. Fluted Doric columns raised on brick piers support the upper and lower porches, contributing to the mansion's elegant ambiance.

Thomas Moore Rhett House has been transformed into an elegant bed and breakfast, the Rhett House Inn.

811 North Street

Some stories claim the charming home at 811 North Street was once a post office, but there is no historical evidence to back this up. Factual evidence dates the rectangular, five-by-two bay frame dwelling to about 1900 or slightly earlier. Much of it is still original, including the hardwood floors throughout. The current owners love the double-tiered porches, which face south and catch the prevailing breeze. When time permits in the lives of two busy professionals who are also new parents, they sit on the upper porch watching tourists amble by and waving to friends.

This wonderful Beaufort home was built around 1900 and restored in 1989.

The owners delight in the many quirky "finds" they have salvaged from trips around the northeast. The dining room glows with the warmth of many candles, lit whenever the couple entertains.

The owners' eclectic taste has won them a huge following of loyal Beaufort shoppers. They run three very successful local businesses where everything from handpainted pottery to baby clothes and freshly cut flowers can be purchased.

The owners salvaged the kitchen cabinet in Pennsylvania, transporting it to Beaufort on top of their car.

The upstairs bedroom is for guests, but will soon be occupied by a growing toddler.

The upstairs porch is a welcome place to relax and enjoy the neighborhood.

Miles Brewton Sams House

801 Prince Street

The Miles Brewton Sams House is believed to have been built by its namesake in 1862. Although it has undergone alterations throughout the years, much of this wonderful home is original. The wooden house faces south, and is raised on brick piers. The main part of the structure is rectangular, with five bays (or windows) across. A two-story, tiered porch on the front of the house

is reconstructed from the original. It replaced an elaborate Victorian-style porch in 1970. The house is now the home of a highly respected local antique dealer and his wife, a commercial airline pilot. They have a keen interest in gardening, and the formal plantings are theirs. They have even planned and maintain a regulation croquet court on the property. Behind the main home is a charming cottage, which they disassembled and moved to this site for use as a guesthouse.

The owner, a respected expert in Southern antiquities, has refined his collection of furnishings with a keen eye toward perfection.

A boxwood hedge camouflages the raised-brick foundation of the Miles Brewton Sams House. The Federal-style porch is a reconstruction placed here in the 1970s. It had been a Victorian rendition that was not in keeping with the antebellum architecture.

Light floods into the kitchen, located on the raised first floor of the home. The small porch just through the doors overlooks a beautiful regulation croquet court.

With meticulous care and planning, the Miles Brewton Sams House has become a showcase for the owner's fine furnishings.

A detail showing the Federal-style mantel.

The historic mansion is home to three very active golden retrievers. On cool days, the upstairs porch is a perfect snoozing place.

Though still elegant, the sitting room on the main floor offers a more relaxed place to entertain.

Miles Brewton Sams House Guesthouse
801 Prince Street

Once a derelict cabin savaged by termites, this cottage behind the Miles Brewton Sams House was dismantled and moved here in the early 1990s to begin a second life as the mansion's guesthouse.

Of perfectly elegant proportions, this tiny house is beloved by the owners and the delighted friends who stay here.

The cottage, as seen from the back porch of the main house.

Every detail has been considered, including where to put wood for the fireplace.

Lined up for spectators, these lawn chairs rest on the edge of the croquet court.

A mixture of cozy antiques and comfortable sofas decorates the cabin.

Water, and references to it, is a part of nearly every Beaufort home.

Wesley United Methodist Church
701 West Street

A granite plaque resting on the wall of the Wesley United Methodist Church states that the congregation was organized in 1833. Experts believe the small, timber-framed vernacular building was built in the 1840s. A Bishop William Capers dedicated it for religious services in 1949. The antebellum structure, renovated in 1985, faces west. Entry is through a three-bay porch supported by four tall, rectangular columns. A vernacular-style tower and pointed spire denote the building's religious purpose.

Wesley United Methodist Church is a marvelous example of vernacular religious structures located throughout the South.

The building is raised on brick piers and has four huge, twelve-over-twelve paned windows on the south side. This is the façade most often seen by residents and tourists, but the main entrance is on West Street.

The interior of the church is simple and elegant.

Only one gravestone lies on the south side of the building; the cemetery is hidden in the shadow of the north side.

William Elliot House, "The Anchorage"

1103 Bay Street

Records dating many of the oldest homes in Beaufort were lost to fire in the Civil War. Historians believe this stately mansion, the William Elliot House, was built about 1800. It is named for William Elliot III, a well-known statesman and entrepreneur of his day. The house was used as a hospital during the Civil War, and was significantly altered by a retired naval officer, Admiral Beardsley, in 1900. Beardsley added stucco to the exterior and ornately carved woodwork in the interior. He replaced a single-story, Federal-style porch with the Corinthian-columned porch we see today. This home owes its present existence to the Historic Beaufort Foundation, which saved it from demolition.

The William Elliot House, also called "The Anchorage," offers sweeping views of the Beaufort River.

1905 North Street

What makes Beaufort such a wonderful walking town is its mix of stately mansions, quaint shops, bustling streets, and quiet canopies of live oak limbs. It is not a museum town frozen in time. Here, the 21st century mixes comfortably with the 18th century. This bungalow, at 1905 North Street, is an example of Beaufort's construction before and after World War I. Showing Craftsman influence, it is a rectangular, one-story frame building with a front-facing gable roof. A young family lives here, decorating with a mix of family antiques, "outsider" art, and funky furniture. This delightful mix provides a lively counterpoint to the mansions of Bay Street, just one block away.

Beaufort's bungalows, built around the turn of the 20th century, were manufactured in quantity. These homes provided inexpensive housing for families, and remain an integral part of the town's livable charm.

Restored to fine condition by the current owners, this home is decorated with furniture and accessories from many eras, giving it a warm and inviting ambiance.

The living room at the front of the house has three-over-one window sashes, a favorite bungalow feature.

40

Sam Doyle was a black artist who lived and worked on St. Helena Island. Painting on found surfaces, most commonly tin, as in the example here, Doyle sold his art from his back yard. Today his paintings hang in museums around the world. The family of the husband/owner collected Doyle's work before it became hugely popular.

The master bedroom is at the back of the home.

41

OLD POINT NEIGHBORHOOD

Lewis Reeve Sams House
601 Bay Street

Built in 1852, the Lewis Reeve Sams House is considered one of the foremost examples of the "Beaufort style" of architecture. Adapted from Greek Revival, the mansion is distinguished on the exterior by its elaborate first- and second-floor entryways: doors surrounded on the sides and tops by narrow bands of rectangular "lights," or panes of glass. The front façade, with its magnificent columned verandahs, overlooks a small park and the Beaufort River beyond.

One of Beaufort's most distinguished mansions, the Lewis Reeve Sams House overlooks the glorious Intracoastal Waterway. The view from both verandahs is wonderful: A constant stream of boats cruises by, piloted by Florida-bound "snowbirds" in the winter, and by coastal waterway enthusiasts year-round. This home, known for years as the Bay Street Inn, was recently restored to a private residence. It is dignified by such extravagant details as marble front steps.

The dining room during renovations. The mansion had been an expensive inn, but was converted back to single-family use in 1999.

Decorative details abound throughout the 19th century mansion. This interior door molding is an example of the elaborate craftsmanship within.

43

William Wigg Barnwell House
501 King Street

Historic accounts suggest that the William Wigg Barnwell House was built in 1815 by the Gibbes brothers on behalf of their sister, Sarah Reeve Gibbes. Sara married William Wigg Barnwell, grandson of the Revolutionary War hero Maj. William Hazzard Wigg. The building served as Union Hospital #4 during the Civil War, and bloodstains are still evident in some of the rooms. In 1973,

this house was slated for demolition, but intervention by the Historic Beaufort Foundation saved it. In September 1973, it was moved several blocks from its original location at 800 Prince Street to its present site on King Street. The man responsible for this work was the legendary Jim Williams of Savannah, whose name was made famous by the book and movie *Midnight in the Garden of Good and Evil.* The magnificent, three-story Federal-style mansion faces south toward the Beaufort River. Its main façade is elegantly appointed with a two-story porch incorporating slender Tuscan columns.

Savannah's legendary Jim Williams moved the magnificent William Wigg Barnwell House to this site in 1973.

The south façade features first- and second-floor porches with tripartite windows to the left and right. A central pediment containing a semicircular louvered ventilation opening surmounts the structure.

A detailed shot of the rich fabrics and antiques that decorate this antebellum mansion.

The owners have been careful to select appropriate antiques to fill the home. Hanging in the front parlor are family photographs and paintings. Jim Williams placed the crystal chandeliers in this room and the dining room. It is said that he intended to keep the fabulous pieces after hanging them to facilitate a quick sale of the house. Instead, the purchasers demanded that they stay with the house and Williams relented.

45

The central hallway of the home, showing the double stairs and rich Federal-style moldings.

The dining room glows with afternoon light. The owners, who entertain frequently, use this room to serve gourmet meals.

This child's bedroom on the third floor is painted with murals depicting famous Confederate heroes. The house served as a hospital during Union occupation of the town.

Elizabeth Hext House, "Riverview"

207 Hancock Street

Built in 1720 as a summer home for Francis Hext, Jr., the Elizabeth Hext House (named for Francis' daughter) is one of the oldest houses in town. Also referred to as "Riverview," this extraordinary home looks out over the Beaufort River from a piece of manicured lawn once called "Black's Point." Riverview has the lofty presence of an antebellum mansion, but is delightfully cozy inside. It stands high in the air on a tabby foundation. A walk through the front door takes you down a short hall and straight out the back to the pool and riverfront dock. Breezes caught in the central hallway are a wonderful form of natural air conditioning, something the original builders no doubt had in mind when positioning the house.

The Elizabeth Hext House takes advantage of one of the nicest lots in Beaufort. The front yard is reached through a wonderful wrought-iron gate. Behind the house is the Beaufort River, also called the Intracoastal Waterway.

A view shows the rear of the house. Originally, the house consisted of upper and lower piazzas, a central hall with flanking rooms on the first floor, and a rear hall and staircase leading to two upstairs bedrooms.

View of the front lawn from the porch.

Gas lanterns and a wrought-iron gate provide wonderful Southern ambiance to the rear of the Elizabeth Hext House.

A reproduction claw-foot tub and pedestal sink stand in a corner of the bedroom.

An upstairs bedroom has a view of the river.

49

Elegant seating in the dining room. The house is decorated with antiques collected by the owners.

Master woodworker William Bosworth used classic design and artistry in building the cabinets when his firm recently remodeled the kitchen of Riverview.

A cozy guest bedroom is tucked downstairs.

William Henry Trescott House
500 Washington Street

William Henry Trescott, who served as assistant secretary of state under President James Buchanan, is said to have built this house on Barnwell Island about 1858, shortly before the Civil War. Col. William Elliot is believed to have dismantled the mansion in 1876, loaded it onto a boat, and reassembled it on Bay Street in Beaufort. There it stayed for nearly 100 years until threatened with demolition in 1975. The Historic Beaufort Foundation came to the rescue, saving the house by moving it onto its present Old Point lot. The raised, two-story house has an unusual eastern orientation—unlike most Beaufort homes that face the river southward. Now a very spacious private home, the Trescott House spent time as an inn after restoration more than twenty years ago.

Entrance at the "back" of the Trescott House leads the visitor up to the raised first floor and through a single-tier porch into the hall. Most informal visitors use the entrance on the south façade, which takes them into the kitchen.

Detail of the stained-glass window in the stairwell between the first and second floors of the house.

An unusually peaceful moment in the living room. The sounds of small moving feet belonging to growing family members or their pets usually stir the air.

Unusual pocket doors fold away into the walls between the dining and living rooms.

Morning light streams into the dining room through the home's many windows. French doors in the background open onto a large porch.

Morning hours are full of activity in the kitchen, where a cheerful sun makes an early entrance.

The huge front porch on the first level of the house is a favorite gathering spot for the family.

One of the French doors that opens into the dining room.

605 Prince Street

The late-Greek Revival details of 605 Prince Street date it to about 1850. It is a good example of the "Beaufort style" of architecture, which combined details from various periods with hot weather-related necessities, such as breeze-facing porches and large windows. In this case, the house has a raised first floor, multiple porches, southern exposure, high ceilings, and a shallow hipped roof. The double porches have chamfered columns, and the main doorway has sidelights and a six-light transom. A black minister, the Reverend Waddell, who served the African Baptist Church around the corner, once lived in the house.

This beautifully-maintained home in the historic district has many elements of the "Beaufort style" of architecture, all intended to help residents cope with the hot climate.

The formal sitting room in the front of the house contains a collection of inherited artwork and antiques.

The owners of the home delight in spontaneous parties, frequently filling the dining room with mouth-watering Southern side dishes and desserts while the oysters steam outside.

All the woodwork and flooring in the house is original, including this mantel in the downstairs sitting room.

The private backyard patio is a peaceful retreat for the busy owners.

Little Taj
401 King Street

This delightful house, nicknamed Little Taj because of the reflection it casts in a neighborhood tidal pool, was built in 1856. Facing south, the structure offers views across the pool and out to the Beaufort River. This perfect orientation allows its residents to enjoy a ·nearly constant breeze. The house is raised on brick piers, with five windows across the front letting in light and air. The main door has sidelights and a transom. The two-story tiered porch is supported by chamfered posts and accentuated by slat balusters.

"Beaufort-style" porches, like those seen on this house at 401 King Street, are not instantly defined by a particular architectural tradition. Each example betrays a range of stylistic influences, since adaptations were unique to local use.

The main entrance from the front porch leads visitors into the hall, from which stairs to the second floor rise.

This charming home is decorated with "child-friendly" antiques and the owners' collection of fine artwork.

A quiet place for a snack or reading a book, while watching neighbors and tourists drift by.

Free of curtains, the Taj's many windows indulge its occupants with light.

The owners are ardent music lovers, as suggested by the much-used piano.

712 East Street

The exact date of construction of this delightful vernacular "cottage" at 712 East Street is unknown, but construction details place it sometime around 1820. Local authorities consider it one of Beaufort's oldest residences. Historical information on many of the town's oldest homes is hard to find, since records were burned during the Civil War. But local lore assigns this home many uses through the years. It may have been a home lived in by relatives of famous citizen Robert Smalls after the Civil War. Less glamorous, it housed returning World War II soldiers and served as a residence for migrant workers. There is also speculation that the house may have been moved at some time from another location.

Renovations, including the enlargement of an interior staircase, took place in the 1960s and a total restoration occurred in the 1980s, when a rear screen porch and a guesthouse were added. Interior work has been substantial, but the home retains its original window and door surrounds, fireplaces, and some of the old windows and window glass. The second floor landing is said to be haunted by a young woman who died in the house and who has protected women in the house by scaring off intruders.

The charming simplicity of this urban cottage beckons to passersby. Neighbors are enticed to stop by for a visit on the porch. The wonderful perennial garden surrounding the home includes period plantings and antique roses, and is lovingly tended by the current owner.

All spring and summer, beautiful pink roses climb over the fence and spill petals onto the residential street seen beyond the white gate.

The rear porch was added during restoration in the 1980s. Behind it, at the end of a brick pathway, is the guest cottage.

The guest cottage has served recently as an apartment for the current owners' young adult children, who love the proximity to home and the privacy it offers.

A corner display in the sitting room off the porch.

Interior decorations reflect the interest and travels of the current owner.

An ivory statue in the living room.

A collection of antique and contemporary Meerschaum pipes is displayed on a table in the dining room.

Despite its beauty, the formal sitting room is often overlooked in favor of cozier rooms toward the rear of the cottage.

Berners Barnwell Sams House (#2)

201 Laurens Street

The construction of this splendid antebellum home around 1852 is attributed to Dr. Berners Barnwell Sams, a local planter and part owner of Datha (now Dataw) Island. It is a magnificent two-story, T-shaped brick structure raised on a high tabby basement. Among the most attention-grabbing details of the home are the massive stucco-covered brick columns at the front. These giant supports are in contrast to the delicate traceried sidelights and transom surrounding the front door and the decorative sawed-timber porch balusters. The home faces a large open field that is locally called "the green." Although it is a part of Sams House property, the grassy area is often a playground for Point residents, and many local children have learned to ride their bikes while circling its soft edges.

The Berners Barnwell Sams House was known as Union Hospital #8 during the Civil War.

The massive unfluted Doric columns make this house appealing and unique.

A delicate garden ornament beckons to admirers from the side yard.

207 Laurens Street

Set back on a sweeping lawn in Beaufort's most historic neighborhood, this delightful raised cottage is immediately loved by all who glimpse it. Said to have been moved as two separate buildings from Coosaw Island, South Carolina, the home dates to about 1875. It recently received the loving attention of new owners, who thoroughly renovated the aging structure and added a separate guesthouse and garage in the back.

The rear entrance to the home leads through a new porch and into the kitchen (with window boxes).

Even on a rainy day, this Lauren Street cottage epitomizes the classic simplicity and friendliness of South Carolina vernacular architecture. The home's huge lawn gives the children and pets of the family plenty of space for outdoor exercise.

The exuberantly painted kitchen table is indicative of the spirit of this high-energy family.

The dining room furnishings are family heirlooms.

The television is cleverly hidden inside the cabinets to the right of
the fireplace in the living room.

From inside the kitchen looking out to the garage/guesthouse
beyond.

John Archibald Johnson House
804 Pinckney Street

Dr. John A. Johnson and his wife, Claudia Talbird, are thought to have built this three-story mansion in the 1850s. It is a raised, two-story brick structure based on a T-shaped plan. The main façade faces south, but the home's entrance is to the east, from marble steps that enter a grand hallway. French doors open onto the gracious porches adorning the house. These are ornamented with unfluted Doric columns on the lower level and fluted columns with Tower of the Winds capitals above. Still in possession of the house at the beginning of the Civil War, Dr. Johnson was ousted and the structure was

used as Union Hospital #3. In 1973, a chimney collapsed, destroying part of a back wall. This led to the eventual issuance of a demolition permit, but the Historic Beaufort Foundation stepped in and purchased the property. Eventually, it was sold to new owners and restored.

In 1999, the present owners created a huge new living space by carving out the basement (or ground level) of the house. The carefully planned and elegantly executed space includes new bedrooms needed in a household raising multiple little ones.

The John Archibald Johnson House at 804 Pinckney Street was almost destroyed in 1974. Thanks to the Historic Beaufort Foundation, the lovely mansion was lovingly restored.

Though the front façade of the house faces south toward the Beaufort River, the entrance is up a set of marble steps on the eastern side of the house. A set of gas lamps adorns the door.

With careful planning, the owners have turned the huge home into a cozy and welcoming place for family and friends.

No room in the house is off limits to children. Although the dining room sparkles with elegance, it is also a great place for hide-and-seek.

French doors open off the living room onto the first-tier porch. Busy children ensure that every inch of the elegant mansion doubles as a playroom.

When the owners recently remodeled the kitchen, they chose woods and cabinet designs to complement the historic space.

A huge new built-in cabinet holds a large-screen television set that can be seen from the kitchen.

Another view of the kitchen, as seen from the television room.

Less formal furnishings dominate in the family rooms at the back of the mansion.

70

Petit Point

505 Washington Street

Hugging the banks of the Beaufort River from its green and leafy lot, this two-story house on the Old Point is always referred to as Petit Point. It is believed that construction dates to about 1855, when it went up to please the tastes of a spinster daughter of the Chaplin family. Perhaps it pleased her as much as it does the visitor today, walking past this charming waterfront home nestled in trees.

The iron gate into the property bears its endearing title.

The lawn at Petit Point is always green, presenting a quaint and idyllic home at the end of a long, brick path.

ST. HELENA ISLAND SITES AND PLANTATIONS

Penn Center
Martin Luther King, Jr. Drive
St. Helena Island

Northern missionaries Ellen Murray and Laura Towne established the Penn Center School on St. Helena Island after Union occupation of the island in 1861 eliminated the practice of slavery. Murray and Towne used education and economic independence to help newly freed blacks become self-sufficient.

Once threatened with a lack of funding and decay, these buildings today are protected and have received grants for restoration and development. On the National Register of Historic Places, Penn Center has a library, museum, school, and church, and many buildings are open for tours.

Truck farming has always provided a means of support for native islanders. Today, the area is being encroached upon by urban development, and as taxes increase, it has become more difficult for landowners to retain their properties. Penn Center has created and fostered community programs helping these family enterprises.

The predecessor to Brick Church at Penn Center on St. Helena Island was a small wooden building erected on what was then John Fripp's Corner Plantation in 1831. In 1855, it was replaced with this grander structure. Attracting slaves and planters, the church swelled with worshippers. The planters abandoned the building when they fled the island in front of advancing Union troops in 1861. From 1862 to 1865, the building housed the Penn School of Ellen Murray and Laura Towne. Brick Church remains an active religious center.

Chapel of Ease Ruins
Martin Luther King, Jr. Drive
St. Helena Island

Sometimes called the "Old White Church," the Chapel of Ease was built in 1740 as an extension of St. Helena's Parish on St. Helena Island. Early planters built the rural church so they could worship without traveling long distances by carriage. They chose a site on Lands End Road (now called Martin Luther King, Jr. Drive) because the path was well traveled by many living on St. Helena Island. At the beginning of the Civil War, about 30 planters owned frontage on the road which passes by the site. Parishioners separated from St. Helena's Parish in the 19th century, and their church became an independent religious site. Considered an outstanding example of early tabby construction, the chapel burned in a forest fire in 1886 and has never been restored. Hollywood came calling at the ruin in the 1980s during the filming of the movie *The Big Chill*.

The walls of the church were constructed of tabby, a local building material comprised of oyster shells, lime, sand, and water. The dignified building is still a place of quiet contemplation.

Seen from a distance, the Chapel of Ease rests on a shady curve of Martin Luther King, Jr. Drive. The site has never been restored, and many fear its continued deterioration.

Holes along the top ridge of the wall are footprints of wooden timbers used to build frames for the tabby mixture. The mixture was poured in sections until the desired height was reached.

Tombee Plantation House

Whooping Crane Lane
St. Helena Island

The oldest existing house on St. Helena Island, this wonderful mansion was built by Thomas B. Chaplin, Sr. around 1795. Tombee (named after its builder, "Thomas B.") reflected the planter's success in the growth of long-staple cotton. The crop was first planted in the Sea Islands about 1790. The house and grounds are idyllically situated above the marsh of pristine Station Creek. It is a remarkable spot. From the drive into the house to the landscaping, there is little to indicate the passage of time. Tombee's high tabby foundation is a huge slab, which lies about four feet underground. Above it, the home, which still sits on its original footprint and has never been moved, is T-shaped, with double-tiered piazzas facing across the marsh. It is so carefully planned that nearly every room receives a steady breeze.

Thomas B. Chaplin kept a detailed journal of plantation life between 1845 and 1858. When he fled St. Helena ahead of the advancing Union army in 1861, he left with little else but the journal. These writings have given historians an insight into antebellum life.

The front of Tombee Plantation House faces Station Creek.

The current owners have meticulously decorated all of the interiors of Tombee with period antiques. The dining room glows from the light of many candles during frequent family gatherings.

Candles are a favorite of the owners, who frequently use them to light the rooms.

A sideboard in the dining room.

Windows in nearly all the rooms catch the prevailing marsh breezes.

The mansion has a commanding presence from the exterior, but is actually quite small on the inside. A set of narrow stairs with original handrail and steps is the only access to the second floor.

The study is directly across the hall from the dining room on the home's main floor.

A comfortable first floor piazza provides a stunning view across Station Creek.

The owners meticulously maintain all of the outbuildings at Tombee. A pear tree decorates the brick walkway with fall bounty.

A view down the driveway shows the guesthouse, which provides comfortable quarters for frequent visitors.

Frogmore Manor

Seaside Road
St. Helena Island

Once a huge Sea Island estate of more than 3,000 acres, Frogmore Manor nearly lost its regal presence to neglect and the severe Sea Island climate. Today, after a thorough restoration in 1996, it has reclaimed its right to be called one of the great antebellum plantation houses in the South. The history of this magnificent site dovetails with the surrounding landscape; it owes its existence to the wealth generated by Sea Island cotton and slavery.

During the mid-18th century, the land was part of the vast holdings of Lt. Gov. William Bull II. A builder from Frogmore, England, built the house about

1810. Around 1855, St. Helena planter Thomas Coffin purchased it. He maintained ownership throughout the turbulent Civil War years. Three years after Coffin died in 1865, Frogmore Manor became home to northern missionaries Ellen Murray and Laura Towne, who established the Penn Center School for newly freed blacks on St. Helena Island. The estate shifted ownership to James Ross McDonald, a prominent St. Helena businessman in the late 19th century. Today, his great-great-granddaughter is rearing her children on the estate. She is the sixth generation of the family to do so.

Facing the grandeur of St. Helena Sound, Frogmore Manor offers its own island as a playground for the owners' children. The Sea Island plantation house is extremely private; a long sandy road leads back into the property.

The house underwent a significant restoration in 1996. Much of the wooden siding had to be replaced, but some of the older boards are still apparent on this western façade.

As with most rooms in this Sea Island mansion, lots of light and air are allowed to move through the dining room.

The view through the front hall of Frogmore Manor. Front and rear doors line up to facilitate island breezes, a natural form of air conditioning.

A television set is cleverly concealed in the cabinet to the right of the fireplace.

The owners have a large collection of family antiques they have used to furnish the house.

A table is set up in the cheerful kitchen for quick family meals.

Although it is difficult to keep sensitive plants thriving in the hot South Carolina climate, the owners have ambitiously started a rose garden in the front yard.

A view across the marsh to St. Helena Sound in the distance.

Land's End Plantation House

Land's End Road
St. Helena Island

The three sprightly towheads who race up and down the private beach that is part of this estate are the second generation of the same family to grow up in this idyllic setting. There is crabbing, fishing, boating, and swimming nearly year-round.

Perfect though this vision may be, however, it is not one that was intended by the designers and builders of this amazing home. When Land's End Plantation House was built on the shores of St. Helena Island in 1898, overlooking St. Helena Sound, it was to serve as an eight-bed military hospital. At the time, the Spanish-American War loomed on the horizon and America was building coastal artillery forts with enthusiasm. This brick structure was built as part of Fort Fremont, a full-scale military operation occupying 176 acres on the island. In 1949, the U.S. government sold the house and twenty acres as military surplus, and private owners converted it into a residence. The solid building had only one bathroom at the time (on the first floor where the bar is today), but subsequent owners went on a bathroom-building binge. There are now ten throughout the four floors.

The current owner marvels at the solid construction of the place, which has never needed structural repair in its 100-year history. Even the roof is original, made from Buckingham County slate said to last 400 years. The walls are four-course thick from top to bottom. Basement walls are cantilevered, adding military-style might to the mansion.

Evening light sets the brick of Land's End Plantation House aglow. The setting sun across St. Helena Sound creates a stunning backdrop for parties in the house. The husband and wife who live here (daughter and son-in-law of the owners) were married here at this time of day, silhouetted against the sky. Now their children play games on the lawn and race down the beach to find shells.

This first floor guest bedroom is full of antiques, including the bed and rugs. Family photographs scattered about create a cozy, welcoming ambiance.

The front hall of the house is painted a bright yellow that turns golden in the late afternoon and evening. The black cabinet seen in the foreground is a piece of "Boule," crafted by Frenchman Henri Boule in the 19th century using elaborate inlays of brass and tortoiseshell.

Two Victorian parlor chairs offer an inviting place to sit with a good book in the family library.

When Land's End was built as a military hospital, this room, now a bar, was the only bathroom in the house. Fewer facilities were needed because the hospital's doctors and nurses did not live in the four-story structure. Today, it houses a collection of antique helmets collected by the son-in-law of the owners. The 85-pound tarpon was caught off Amelia Island, Florida, some years ago.

Another view of the library, showing the wood stove that helps to heat the big mansion during the winter. Bookshelves display family heirlooms and memorabilia.

The huge living room on the first floor is filled with all manner of comfortable antique furniture. Some are precious and some not. This is where the huge family Christmas tree is placed, and local children are invited over for holiday cheer at the beach.

A view across the lawn to the beach. Family members and guests often share a glass of wine while pausing to enjoy the glorious view.

There are few views anywhere in the world to rival this one, from the beach at Land's End Plantation House.

Coffin Point Plantation House

Coffin Point Drive
St. Helena Island

Built in 1800, Coffin Point Plantation House rests on a wide lawn that provides a view across Port Royal Sound and the Atlantic Ocean. The foundation is made of tabby, an early Sea Island building material comprised of lime, sand, and oyster shells. A beautiful example of Federal-style architecture, the house is enhanced by cornice-line dentils (front façade; rear façade shown). The roof is hipped with central pediment and dormer windows at each end. The main doorway is semi-elliptical, and the door to the upper porch has side and fan lights.

Ebenezer Coffin built Coffin Point and kept elaborate journals of plantation life. One of his 1800 entries specified that he had hired carpenters to "work in St. Helena in erecting a dwelling, stable and negro house." The Coffins were among the Sea Island plantation families who fled in front of advancing Union troops in 1861. They never returned. After emancipation, the home became headquarters for the Port Royal Experiment, teaching newly freed slaves to read and write.

Coffin Point Plantation House.

SHELDON AND PLANTATIONS OF PORT ROYAL SOUND

George Edwards House
Tabby Ruins
Spring Island

Spring Island, a 2,000-acre sea island located about thirteen miles southeast of Beaufort, is surrounded by the waters of the Chechessee and Colleton rivers, and Chechessee Creek. Now an exclusive residential development, the primitive island was granted to John Cockran, an Indian trader, on September 1, 1706. He never lived here, however, and his son, James, made the first improvements sometime before his death in 1739.

George Edwards acquired Spring Island at the beginning of the 19th century. Cotton was the major cash crop of the plantation and slavery the means to this wealth. Tabby ruins are all that remain of a large home built sometime before 1800. Tabby, a mixture of lime made from oyster shells, whole shells, sand, and water, was a favorite medium for residential structures of the time. The few remaining examples scattered across the Low Country are regarded as archeological treasures.

The ruins shown in these photographs are of a house and dependencies built in two phases. At first, the structure was probably rectangular, two stories high, with end chimneys and a gable roof. Sometime early in the 19th century, the Edwards House underwent enlargement, including the addition of two tabby wings flanking the main house. The federal government in 1861 confiscated it. It was abandoned and vandalized during the Civil War.

Spring Island Development Corporation has gone to great lengths to study and conserve the tabby ruins of the George Edwards House, protecting them from further decay. These magnificent archeological remains are situated overlooking the water, arrived at through a sand path beneath a bower of live oaks.

Builders created tabby structures by pouring the mixture into wooden frames the length and thickness of the walls. These forms had no bottoms, but the sides were joined at intervals by wooden braces. Square holes in the walls show the footprints of early manufacturing techniques.

Now a memory, the early house was made of tabby. Conservation efforts are apparent in door and window frames, and along the tops of the walls.

On a bright day, shadows playfully mimic the shapes of the ruins on surrounding grass.

In the spring, a profusion of wild irises blooms along the sand road leading to the site.

Prince William's Church Ruins, Sheldon Ruins

Old Sheldon Church Road

Brick columns, which still stand, display a sense of the classic proportions of the original structure.

Yemassee Indians once inhabited the land upon which this magnificent ruin now stands. Chased into Florida after a bloody conflict in 1715, the Indians surrendered the territory to planter colonists, who began settling the area. By 1745, there were enough plantations here to warrant the establishment of a local church separate from St. Helena's in Beaufort. And there was wealth enough to ensure that it would be impressive. Prince William's Church was finished in 1753. Unfortunately, it did not stand for long. In 1779, British forces planning an attack on Charleston came upon the structure and burned it to the ground. Planters rebuilt the church in 1862, only to see their efforts destroyed when General Sherman's 15th Corps burned the structure in 1865.

The ruins of Prince William's Church are known locally as "Old Sheldon." This quiet place, draped in Spanish moss and Gothic beauty, draws hundreds of visitors annually. Many come just to walk and absorb the aura of this spiritual spot. Others join annual church services held by the congregation of St. Helena's Episcopal Church, which owns the spot.

Services, including many marriages, are still held at the ruin. The serene atmosphere of this remote site lends a certain Southern-Gothic solemnity.

The impressive tombs of John and Mary Bull are in the graveyard at the Sheldon ruins. The Bulls were nearby plantation owners and helped establish the church. John Bull's first wife was a victim of the Yemassee Indian War of 1715, and she is remembered as being "carried off by the Indians." The inscription on the tomb of Mary Bull reads: "Within this tomb lie the remains of Mary Bull, wife of John Bull, a much loved and lamented parent, who died November 19, 1771."

Tomotley Plantation,
Avenue of Oaks
Old Sheldon Church Road

The spectacular avenue of 200-year-old live oaks at Tomotley Plantation is one of the most breathtaking natural sites in the state of South Carolina. The land that is now Tomotley was once part of a 13,000-acre land grant established in the beginning of the 18th century. The Izard family of Goose Creek cut Tomotley Plantation out of the original acreage in 1755. But it wasn't until sometime around 1820 that Patience W.B. Izard, wife of Abraham Eustis and the last Izard owner of Tomotley, planted the magnificent avenues of trees that radiate from the site of her house.

The main entrance to Tomotley Plantation is just down the road from the ruins of Old Sheldon Church. The magnificent vista through the live oak trees teases the eye with what might lie beyond. There is no antebellum mansion on the grounds; the present home is a grand replica patterned on traditional Southern design.

The live oak "allee" (or avenue) at Tomotley was planted nearly 200 years ago by Patience Izard.

Stoney Creek Independent Presbyterian Church

McPhersonville Church Road
McPhersonville

Stoney Creek Independent Presbyterian Church was established on May 20, 1743, when a call was issued to the Rev. William Hutson to become the pastor of a church in McPhersonville, South Carolina. This beautiful chapel was built circa 1832-1833 on Stoney Creek near Pocotaligo. Used as a hospital for wounded soldiers during the Civil War, Stoney Creek Chapel was the only structure in Jasper County to survive the torches of the 15th Corps of General Sherman's army, commanded by Maj. Gen. John A. Logan, as it crossed into South Carolina from Savannah, Georgia, in 1865. It is the only antebellum building to survive in McPhersonville.

Small but proud, this regal little church sits at the end of a rural road in Jasper County. It received the attention of Hollywood a few years ago when it was used during the filming of the movie Forrest Gump.

Round-headed windows and matching shutters add to the considerable charm of this vernacular, Greek Revival church. Other period details—Tuscan columns and front-gabled roof, common features of this architectural style—add to its Greek-temple-like appearance.

Sheldon Episcopal Chapel
McPhersonville Church Road
McPhersonville

Early planters who worshipped at Prince William's Church in Sheldon first built a "chapel of ease" on this picturesque country site in 1831. Episcopalians living in what is now the upper part of Hampton County were too far from the formal parish church at Sheldon. Instead of traveling, they attended this cool country retreat during long, hot South Carolina summers. Church members added a gallery for black worshippers in 1837. During the Civil War, members of the Confederate army converted it into a hospital for smallpox patients. General Sherman's troops destroyed the original building on January 30, 1865. Episcopal worship services are still held in this charming structure, rebuilt in 1898, at special times.

At the first service on this spot after the Civil War ended, congregates read from Psalm 84: "How lovely is your dwelling place, O Lord of hosts! My soul longs, indeed it faints for the courts of the Lord; my heart and my flesh sing for joy."

This side elevation of the Sheldon Chapel in McPhersonville displays charming, Gothic Revival details, such as pointed-arch windows with matching shutters. Brick piers, such as those shown here raising the structure off the ground, are common architectural elements throughout the Carolina "Low Country," where marshy soil and termites abound.

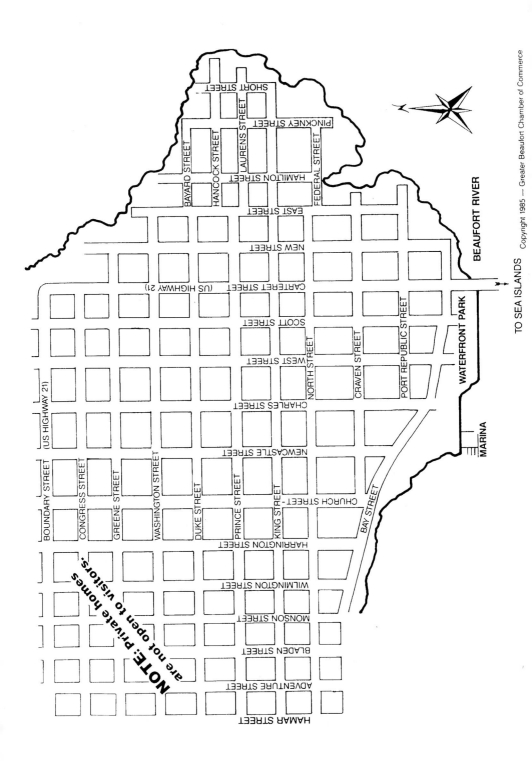

NOTE: Private homes are not open to visitors.

BOUNDARY STREET (US HIGHWAY 21)
CONGRESS STREET
GREENE STREET
WASHINGTON STREET
DUKE STREET
PRINCE STREET
KING STREET
CHURCH STREET
BAY STREET

HAMAR STREET
ADVENTURE STREET
BLADEN STREET
MONSON STREET
WILMINGTON STREET
HARRINGTON STREET
NEWCASTLE STREET
CHARLES STREET
WEST STREET
SCOTT STREET
CARTERET STREET (US HIGHWAY 21)
NEW STREET
EAST STREET

BAYARD STREET
HANCOCK STREET
LAURENS STREET
PINCKNEY STREET
HAMILTON STREET
FEDERAL STREET
SHORT STREET

NORTH STREET
CRAVEN STREET
PORT REPUBLIC STREET

WATERFRONT PARK
MARINA

BEAUFORT RIVER

TO SEA ISLANDS   Copyright 1985 — Greater Beaufort Chamber of Commerce